God's Beauty of Nature

Tina Hassan

Archway Publishing books may be ordered through booksellers or by contacting:

Archway Publishing
1663 Liberty Drive
Bloomington, IN 47403
www.archwaypublishing.com
844-669-3957

Interior Image Credit: Tina Hassan

ISBN: 978-1-6657-1842-4 (sc)
ISBN: 978-1-6657-1843-1 (e)

Library of Congress Control Number: 2022901800

Print information available on the last page.

Archway Publishing rev. date: 02/01/2022

God's Beauty of Nature

~Winter Wonderland~

Waking up to a winter wonderland full of snow,
What a beautiful morning, looking out my bedroom window,
Witnessing the tree covered in a blanket of snow,
As the doves look at each other and coo.

Like the innocence of a child everything is pure and white,
Calm and peaceful,
Enjoying this lovely morning feeling the sunlight,
As I open the window to let in the cool breeze, I feel free and grateful.

Cuddling with my cat,
Eating a Kit-Kat,
With a book in my hand,
It's picture perfect in my own backyard looking like a winter wonderland.

~Appreciate this Day~

Waking up early one morning,
To the sound of birds chirping and singing,
As I step out onto the balcony – looking up to the sky and see a cloud in the shape of a heart,
Capturing a photo - before it splits apart.

Taking this day to appreciate,
Even though I'm running late,
I'm about to appreciate this day,
It's the little things we take for granted but no more - starting from today.

Telling loved ones how much I love and appreciate them,
We're too busy looking for better things when we already have our special gems,
Let's do this every day,
And appreciate this God given day.

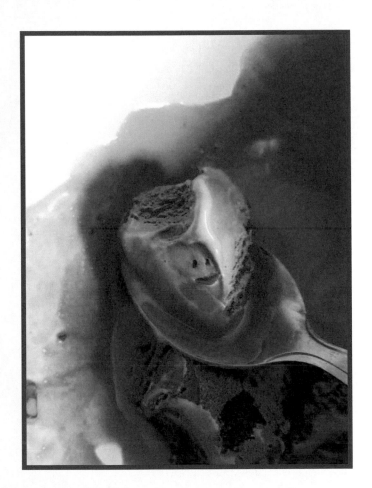

~Sweet Day~

As I sit to relax and unwind,
I thought I was losing my mind,
Eating a bowl of ice cream,
I know this is not a dream.

Before I take a bite, I notice a smiley face on my spoon,
Chocolate chips as eyes and a wicked
smile in a shape of a moon,
I reach for the camera and take a quick photo,
I take several shots back to back as I have it set on auto.

A reminder that no matter what kind
of day I'm going through,
I can always have coffee set for later on brew,
While I enjoy eating my ice cream like today,
Oh, what a sweet day!

~The Lonely Flower~

Out for a hike on a gorgeous day,
I do my stretches first, I must say,
I looked down and in front of me is a lonely flower,
I look up and I see a tower.

The lonely flower all alone,
In the field standing out strong,
Having all the power that she owns,
With her roots is where she belongs.

~Driving off into the Sunset~

What a beautiful night,
I'll bet to see it would be a delight,
Above the waters and over the bridge,
My phone vibrates and I spilled coffee on me, by a smidge.

I pull over to the side of the road,
After passing a truck full of load,
So many mistakes I'll admit,
But I'll need this photo tonight to submit.

Everything is fine,
All I need is a glass of wine,
Driving off into the Sunset,
With my child and nothing to regret.

~The Dancing Sun~

Having a rough day, join the club,
I make myself a twelve-foot sub,
I heard sad news today,
It just ruined my day.

I just wanted to curl up and cry,
Instead I make a sandwich and let out a sigh,
I stand outside as I take a bite,
Looking up to the sky and thought I saw a kite.

Nope, it's just the sun and looks like it's dancing,
Neighborhood kids laughing and playing,
A sign to be happy and dance away the blues,
Like the dancing sun as one of the many given clues.

~Day at the Beach~

A quiet day at the beach,
Today I shall not preach,
Going to relax and get some sun,
With my son just having fun.

We have it all to ourselves,
Already set up two umbrellas,
Day at the beach to relax and unwind,
Thirteen missed calls but paying no mind.

Listening to the sound of the splashing waves,
To having picnics and getting a tan,
Later, we jump over the waves,
Then ending the day making sand castles and being greeted by a fan.

~The Shining Moon~

One dark night,
There it was up above so high a bright light,
Everyone was asleep,
The shining moon stands out without making a peep.

Behind a tree,
Where one can still see,
Between the tree branches and leaves of summer green,
Yet not to be hidden.

Not a full moon,
But a half moon,
Not a yellow moon
But a bright, white light, guiding us, is the shining moon.

~A Day Out on The Boat~

Picture a perfect day,
Today is that day,
White puffy clouds, blue skies,
No sounds of baby cries.

Peaceful and quiet,
Sunny day and about to break my diet,
Going out deep and just think,
With lots of snacks and a nice cold drink.

A day to remember,
Snacking on a cucumber,
A day out on a boat,
Not having to wear a coat.

~Lion in My Coffee~

What's this? Lion in my coffee, *Oh My!*
I give it a swirl, and release a sigh,
Never have I ever seen a lion in my coffee,
Very pleasing to see, wouldn't you agree.

Here I am sitting on my couch,
Curled up with a good book,
Cuddling with my cat with a soft touch,
Hearing a knock at the door
and it's my friend Brooke.

We talk about the book and drink coffee,
I tell her about the lion in my coffee,
We laugh about it as we sip,
Later heading out to the lake for a dip.

~The Praying Tree~

Driving around on a cloudy day,
We witness strange things that we can't explain,
Had I told you, would you had believed what I say,
Probably not, so here's a photo from after the rain.

A tree caught in between the wires,
Or perhaps it's just a praying tree,
I've seen and heard of wild forest fires,
Windows down as I drive by and I get kissed by a bee.

I say you don't forget a tree like this,
They say you don't forget a pretty face,
What a bliss,
Come on now, let's fully embrace.

~The Red Tree Leaves~

One sunny morning,
On our way to Six Flags Fiesta,
Stopping at rest area in Texas in
front of the red tree leaves,
A gorgeous tree, I had to take this
shot as I rolled up my sleeves.

How blessed to be parked in front
of this amazing tree,
The red tree leaves rustling,
Feeling free,
Along with the gentle wind as if it was dancing.

~The Bare Tree~

Oh what a misty day,
Going out for a hike,
Along the trails in Mid-May,
Beautiful scenery I do like.

Standing strong before me is the bare tree,
Still misty out and the sky is gray,
We reach the mountaintop and I take
a sip of my peppermint tea,
Adam sits upon a rock and I nod
in agreement to stay.

Staring at the spectacular scenery,
While sitting beside the bare tree,
Not much greenery,
Still an awesome day to get out and see.

~Waterfall~

Beautiful drive out to nowhere,
Parked and got out the car,
Going on a long hike must lead to somewhere,
A gorgeous sight to see from afar.

I can hear kids laughing,
And birds chirping,
It starts to drizzle and passing by is a crow,
The rain stops and I witness a double rainbow.

As I get closer I can hear the sound of a waterfall,
As I get closer I take a picture,
A breathtaking view surrounded by
trees that are strong and tall,
If only I was quick enough to snap
it with the rainbow mixture.

~Lusciousness~

Full and rich in color,
The vibrant of green,
The lusciousness - to see it is an honor,
Even as a teen.

Different heights of the lusciousness green trees,
The lusciousness green grass,
Another day to seize,
Not a day to waste or let this pass.

Getting fresh air,
Taking a short drive,
Playing truth or dare,
There are no bees, but we sure did see a beehive.

~Hues of the Blue & Green Sea~

Hues of the blue and green sea,
Glistening like sparkling cider,
Son, it's just you and me,
Later we can ride on our wave rider.

Feeling the soft sand as we walk barefoot,
And the hues of blue and green sea splashing us,
Time to change into our bathing suit,
And catch the shuttle bus.

~Sunset~

The day has come to an end,
The sun is setting,
The beautiful colors of sunset blend,
Just a few hours ago people were at the horse race betting.

It's not everyday you get to see the same sunset,
For now enjoy this evening and be grateful,
This morning you may have woken up upset,
We have many blessings in life but are never thankful.

Whatever you're going through,
Tomorrow is another day,
I have a little cold just glad its not the flu,
Going off to bed after I pray.

~Above the Clouds~

(photo credit - Adam Kasht)

Flying from KS City MO to Cancun, Mexico,
Landing at the Atlanta Georgia airport before switching planes,
My son is texting his friend Ronaldo,
Telling him we are on the plane while
handing me a candy-cane.

Up above the clouds we go,
So high in the sky,
We looked down and then we shook our head saying *oh no,*
Flying like a soaring eagle - *oh my.*

The clouds look soft and puffy,
The color of clouds are pure white,
A lady sitting behind me talking about her dog Muffy,
Above the clouds - sunny and bright.

~Above the Sea~

(photo credit - Adam Kasht)

Flying above the glistening sea,
Asking for orange juice,
Instead I get a cup of tea,
Not complaining but rather feeling bliss,

Landing in Atlanta and eating chicken at Popeyes,
Back to boarding on plane,
Off to Mexico and hearing lots of sighs,
I'm writing as I stare out the window pane.

No longer above the sea,
Landing in Mexico,
Grabbing a cup of coffee,
And out the door we go.

~The Golden Heart Leaf~

What a marvelous sight,
Talk about standing out from the crowd,
All the leaves are green except one that is bright,
A single golden heart shaped leaf - silenced yet - LOUD.

It is not proud,
Stands out shining,
As the sun shines passing through a puffy cloud,
Blue Jay lands on a tree branch and starts singing.

A cardinal joins as well as a red robin,
Together they make a beautiful sound,
I capture a photo of the shiny leaf and then go in,
While picking up a lucky coin from the ground.

~Gloomy Day~

Oh the storm is coming,
The sky is sad,
I'm over here humming,
Singing away the blues - nope, I'm not mad.

I'm just glad I'm not out stuck somewhere,
Just home where I belong,
Listening to sounds of rustling winds
coming from everywhere,
It's a gloomy day but still I'm
humming and singing along.

Not a cloud in the sky,
Not even the sun trying to force its way out,
Up above the sky so high,
It's so peaceful and quiet - until my
neighbor's kids started to pout!!

~Sherbert Sky~

Rise N' Shine,
A gorgeous sky,
No time to whine,
I see a colorful sherbert sky - *"Oh My!"*

I reach quick for my camera,
And click I snap,
Sent to my friend Sarah,
She called me and my phone died - *"crap!"*

While I'm charging my phone,
She has now told many about it,
It's been posted on Facebook - *"OUCH!"*
I hit my elbow and got a funny bone,
My phone came back on and so
far got a millions view hit.

~Sweet Red~

So, I went and got my nails done today,
Then off to store and bought some sweet chocolates,
Who knew that the colors of my nails and chocolates would be sweet red - oh what a fine day,
The colors match perfectly - so bright in red - looking classy and elegant in my black stilettos.

My friends thought I was shooting for a commercial,
HA! If only, that would had been amazing,
What a shocker it would be - hence one may have to be punctual,
All eyes on me as everyone is now starring.

No, I'm not a famous celebrity,
But who knows maybe one day,
Money and fame means nothing it's all about integrity,
Just posting a photo of a perfect sweet day.

Celebrating life and the sweetness,
The ups and downs,
The sourness and bitterness,
Smiles and frowns.

~Purple Water Fountain~

The magical water fountain with a touch of purple,
How it rises and gives it a magic touch,
Looking at it beautifully as it makes a ripple,
Getting my camera that's attached to my hip in my pouch.

I take a picture,
The sun is setting,
I can hear someone behind me getting a lecture,
They're arguing from earlier today about the betting.

I'm enjoying watching the purple water fountain in front of me,
Just glaring,
A grande to see,
If you were wondering.

~The Sun and the Moon~

How blessed to see both the sun and the moon,
Together in the sky,
So close yet distant in the month of June,
Setting on the left is the sun way up high.

Rising on the right is the moon,
Sitting by the lake,
Reading a book till noon,
Having a glass of wine and a piece of cake.

~Sweet November~

Sweet November, how I love you,
The month of being thankful,
The colors of rainbow,
Mainly pink and red. I'm always grateful.

Sweet November, the sun shining through,
On a clear blue sky,
Leaves changing colors before you,
How lovely to see green leaves and red leaves to pink sky and blue sky.

~Spotting A Rainbow~

A sign that there's always hope,
Here I was sitting on the couch,
Moping around until I looked up and said nope,
I felt someone's touch.

All my sadness and pain went away,
I spotted a rainbow behind the tree,
I smile and jump up from the couch to dance away,
Music on blast feeling happy and free.

My phone rings,
I let it go to voicemail.
I spotted a rainbow and my phone once again dings,
I received an email.

Feeling the blues were temporary,
Once I spotted a rainbow,
On the contrary,
I thought it was all because of you!

About the Author

Tina Hassan is a faith-filled traveler, photographer, and writer who travels globally to capture phenomenal images and blend them with poems so that others may witness and enjoy the beauty of nature gifted to us by God.

About the Book

As I sit to relax and unwind,
I thought I was losing my mind,
Eating a bowl of ice cream,
I know this is not a dream.
Before I take a bite, I notice a smiley face on my spoon,
Chocolate chips as eyes and a wicked smile in a shape of a moon,

By taking a moment to look around and appreciate the little things we take for granted, we can easily see the beauty, appreciate each day, and know that God is always beside us on our walks through life.

Tina Hassan intertwines poems with original photos of sunsets, sunrises, lakes, waterfalls, and even ice cream as she vividly captures the many gifts that life provides on a daily basis. Her reflections and images touch on a variety of subjects that include a lonely flower in a field, a drive into the sunset, a day on a boat, the red leaves of an amazing tree, the hues of a blue and green sea, a purple water fountain, and much more.

God's Beauty of Nature shares a visual artist's perspective of our beautiful world through original photographs and poems that capture the everyday gifts He provides.

Printed in the United States
by Baker & Taylor Publisher Services